# THE BIG BOOK OF PIRATES

THE BIG BOOK OF

# PIRATES

By Chuck Tessaro

Illustrated by Anatoly Slepkov

COURAGE BOOKS

AN IMPRINT OF RUNNING PRESS
PHILADELPHIA • LONDON

Printed in China

9  8  7  6  5  4  3  2  1
Digit on the right indicates the number of this printing

Library of Congress Control Number: 2004103988

ISBN 0-7624-1624-6

Cover and Interior designed Matt Goodman
Edited by Elizabeth Encarnacion
Typography: Nofret and Caslon Antigue

This book may be ordered by mail from the publisher.
***But try your bookstore first!***

Published by Courage Books, an imprint of
Running Press Book Publishers
125 South Twenty-second Street
Philadelphia, Pennsylvania 19103-4399

Visit us on the web!
www.runningpress.com

# TABLE OF
# CONTENTS

# WHAT ARE PIRATES?

When you think of the word pirate, a picture may come to your mind. You might imagine a ruthless-looking, sea-crusted sailor with leathery brown skin and a black patch covering one eye. The pirate may be wielding a razor-sharp cutlass and smoking pistol, traveling aboard a sleek wooden ship poised to attack a merchant vessel, in the hopes of seizing the ultimate booty—treasure chests brimming with gold, silver, jewels, and untold riches.

This image of a pirate is partly true. The term pirate simply means "robber of the sea," someone whose sole purpose in life is to attack and take things from other ships. Most pirates of old did use sharp cutlasses, daggers, and pistols, and many wore scarves around their heads. These barbaric brutes stole hoards of goods from others, including gold, silver, jewelry, money, tools, food, weapons, textiles, and supplies. Sometimes they even kept the ships they attacked!

The pirate lifestyle attracted people for many reasons. Some turned to piracy because they wanted a life of adventure and an opportunity to obtain vast riches. Others were former government sailors who traded a life of strict rules and order for the democracy and sense of belonging that many pirate ships offered. Many were licensed by governments to raid enemy ships. Whatever their reasons for becoming pirates, their lives have fascinated people for hundreds of years.

## ❧ EARLY SEA ROBBERS ❧

Pirates have been plundering the seas for thousands of years, dating back to when ships were first built for transporting and trading goods. Even the great ancient civilizations of Greece and Rome were concerned about pirates attacking their ships and stealing valuable goods like wine, wheat, and olive oil. Over 2,000 years ago, pirates in swift galleys attacked from the many protected small islands that dot the coastline of Greece, waiting in hidden coves for trade ships to pass. They would oar their boats and quickly overcome large and bulky sail-driven merchant ships. Alexander the Great (356–323 BC), who ruled over Greece, worried about pirate attacks and attempted to clear the pirates from the seas to create safer passages for trade ships. When these early pirates weren't attacking on the Aegean Sea, they went on shore and pillaged small towns and villages along the coast, forcing people to move far inland.

## ❧ PRIVATEERS ❧

Privateers were legal pirates who were hired or given a license called a Marque of Letters, by their governments. This license gave them the right to steal from or destroy enemy ships and perform other tasks for the government that employed them. In a way they were good pirates, because they were hired to protect their countries from hostile ones. France and England were famous for using privateers, ordering them to attack and steal the cargoes of enemy ships. American privateers were used to support the American navy in the War for Independence.

A captain was commissioned, given a Marque, and was expected to recruit and train the crew, then carry out special orders given by the government. The captain and crew of a privateer would receive part of any plundered loot, and

was common for them to treat their prisoners cruelly. Most of the buccaneers were French sailors who had settled there because they were no longer interested in living a life at sea. Some were former privateers whose licenses had been taken away by England's government in an effort to stop the raids in the Spanish Main. Others were escaped slaves

> On Hispaniola, the buccaneers lived lawlessly as free men, hunting animals like wild pigs and cattle. They dried and cured their meat in BOUCANS, a type of smoke-house. This is the origin of the name "buccaneer."

the government would keep the rest. In exchange, the hosting government would provide a safe haven for the privateers when they weren't sailing the high seas and attacking the enemy. Privateers often did not follow the letter of the law, though. They sometimes went far beyond the orders of the government who hired them and did things they had no official right to do, such as attacking and plundering ships that belonged to countries who were not their enemies.

## ❧ BUCCANEERS ❧

When Christopher Columbus and the conquistadors of Spain settled in the Americas (dubbed "The New World"), they found great riches and resources such as gold and silver, much of which was shipped back to Europe. The Spanish conquered and ruled much of these lands, and they became known as the Spanish Main. The Spanish Main lured pirates and privateers who wanted a piece of the riches that were continually sailing back to Europe from the Americas.

On the island of Hispaniola, in the Caribbean, lived the buccaneers. They were considered a brutal bunch, and it

and convicts. These men from different backgrounds banded together because the Spanish were trying to drive them off the island of Hispaniola.

At first, the buccaneers could easily attack the Spanish ships, called galleons. The galleons were heavy, well-built wooden ships, most with more than 50 cannons and 200 men to defend them. Galleons sailed quite slowly due to their great size and weight, and the buccaneers would approach in smaller vessels, trying to avoid a direct attack. After sneaking up on the ship, they would shoot at the hapless crew members with long muskets. Eventually, the Spanish learned to thwart these attacks by sailing in large groups of ships.

## ❧ MAROONERS ❧

Pirates lived by strict rules, or Codes of Conduct, that outlined what they could and could not do. A pirate ship was run like a democracy, where majority vote established the rule. When a pirate committed a serious crime, oftentimes he was "marooned," or put ashore on a deserted island. Marooning was a harsh punishment. The unlucky pirate would be left alone on an island far removed from the general population. Sometimes they gave him a bottle of water and a gun with a few bullets, but excluding these few supplies, he was left to survive on only his wits. His only chance of survival would be to flag down a passing ship; however, legend has it that pirates that were marooned usually died. Members of the crew weren't the only ones who were punished this way. Even a captain could be marooned for waging poor attacks, inadequately providing for his crew, or making bad decisions.

The marooners were 17th century pirates who cruised the Atlantic coast of North America, the coast of Africa, and the West Indies, attacking and plundering passing ships. The marooners were a diverse group from many different nations with a common cause—to rob the seas. Unlike the buccaneers, who attacked Spanish ships and settlements exclusively, the marooners attacked ships from any nation, seeking out cargoes such as grain and tobacco from merchant ships traveling from New England and along the coast.

# WHERE DID PIRATES PLUNDER?

Pirates have plundered most of the world's seas. During the Golden Age of Piracy, they were most active in the Caribbean. Here was the Spanish Main—the route by which the Spanish took gold, silver, and other riches from the Americas. When piracy in the Spanish Main died down, pirates moved to the Indian Ocean, where trade between the East and Europe was expanding. In North America, pirates attacked British merchant and navy ships, helping America secure its independence. Wherever there was loot to steal, pirates could be found. Today, one of the most popular places for piracy is the South China Sea.

## ❋ PIRATES OF THE MEDITERRANEAN ❋

During the era of the ancient civilizations of Greece and Rome, pirates had success plundering the Mediterranean because there were so many trading vessels in a relatively small body of water. The Mediterranean also offered many excellent hiding places on the many islands and in secluded coves all along the coastlines.

Between the 11th and 17th centuries, there were two groups of pirates who waged a religious war. These were the Christian corsairs from the island of Malta, and the Muslim corsairs from the north coast of Africa. The Muslim corsairs were known as the Barbary pirates because they operated along the Barbary Coast of Africa, including the areas of Algiers, Tripoli, and Tunis. The Barbary corsairs had oared galleys with over one hundred fighting men, but these men didn't do any of the rowing—that was left to slaves. When the Barbary corsairs boarded a Christian merchant ship, they treated the enemy crew harshly, causing great pain and suffering. They immediately turned them into slaves and stole their ships. These prisoners were commonly shackled together while rowing long oars to power the ship, and didn't survive for long. Some lucky slaves might be released if their families paid an expensive ransom. The Christian corsairs of Malta treated captured Barbary corsairs the same way. When these two pirate groups were not attacking each other, they were plundering trade ships from other countries.

## ❋ THE SPANISH MAIN ❋

The Spanish Main was the most legendary stage for pirates thirsty for riches and adventure. Beginning in the late 15th century, Spain set out to find a more convenient trade route to the East. What they found were the Americas, vast lands rich with treasure not found in Europe. The Spanish conquistadors found gold and jewels in parts of Mexico and South America. The Spanish explorers established settlements and mined the riches for transport back to Europe. Many argue that pirates were a ruthless bunch, but the Spanish conquistadors were thieves also. It was the Spanish army that ultimately attacked and wiped out the ancient civilizations of the Americas, including the Aztecs

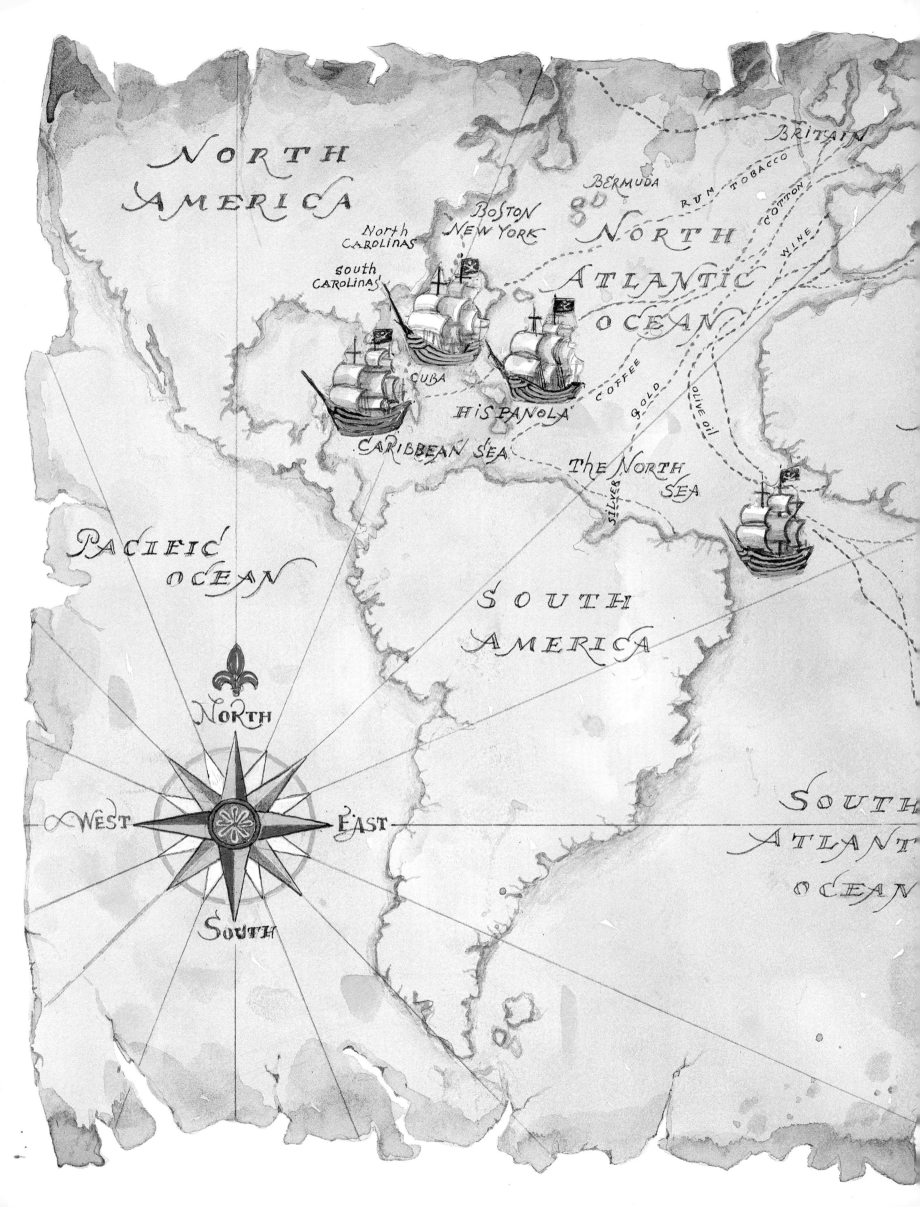

and Incas, by the beginning of the 16th century.

The Spanish Main consisted of North and South America and later included the Caribbean Sea and the

attack merchant vessels heading for Europe. The actions of the pirates in the Far East crippled the area's trade with Europe.

> One famous female pirate who raided the South China Seas and the Pearl River Delta was Cheng I Sao, or Madame Cheng. She consolidated different pirate gangs in the area, and built a pirate fleet of more than 2,000 ships and thousands of men and women under her command.

surrounding islands in the West Indies such as Jamaica and Hispaniola. After the Spanish had set up colonies and plundered the gold and silver from the Americas, they sailed it back Europe on enormous treasure ships, called galleons. The pirates in the Spanish Main sailed in small, sleek sloops, which were swift and easy to maneuver to catch up with the treasure ships sailing to Europe. This period, known as the Golden Age of piracy, included the time period between the 16th and 18th centuries, but mainly the 30 years before 1725.

## ❋ PIRATES OF THE FAR EAST ❋

For centuries, pirates have scoured the Indian Ocean and South China Seas, seeking out booty from trading ships carrying luxuries and goods. In the late 17th century, piracy in the Spanish Main was dwindling, and pirate activity in the East began to heat up. Trade was growing in the East, especially where merchants from East India Companies hauled valuable treasure like silk, spices, porcelain, and tea across the Indian Ocean and Red Sea. Arab and Indian pirates attacked them using vessels called *dhows*, which were small and sleek. They, along with pirates from the Americas, cruised across the Atlantic Ocean to the south of Africa near Madagascar, which was a prime staging area for pirates to

In the South China Seas, convoys of pirates sailed in boats called junks. They weren't what the name suggests— on the contrary, they were strong vessels that were really converted merchant ships that had been fortified with extra guns and crew. Junks were fairly narrow ships with three masts, and part of the rigging was made of bamboo. They were highly decorative ships and flew flags different from the Jolly Rogers hoisted by the pirates of the Spanish Main. During this time, pirate junks were almost unstoppable. The Chinese and Japanese navies joined forces in an effort to halt the plundering, but they had too few warships to do much.

## ❋ PRIVATEERS OF AMERICA ❋

One of the most powerful groups of pirates was the American privateers used during the American Revolution (1775–1783). America was trying to establish its independence from British rule, and it used pirates to help win the fight for freedom. Hundreds of pirates were recruited as privateers and given Marques by the fledgling government in return for swearing allegiance to American independence. These volunteer pirates were paid excellent wages to attack British merchant vessels in the Atlantic Ocean and West Indies, disrupting Britain's lucrative trade routes. These brave privateers also protected their own waters along the North American coast. They chased English ships on the high seas, capturing supplies that were difficult to find during the war, like weapons, ammunition, and food. Some were lucky enough to intercept and loot cargoes containing precious booty like gold!

After a brief period, privateers were again called upon during another war with Britain in 1812. The events leading up to the war were complicated, with America having disputes with Canada, and the British struggling against both France and America. The French imposed a European blockade against English ships, and the British in turn seized American ships and forced the crews to serve in the Royal Navy. During this war, American privateers again successfully attacked and captured British merchant and warships.

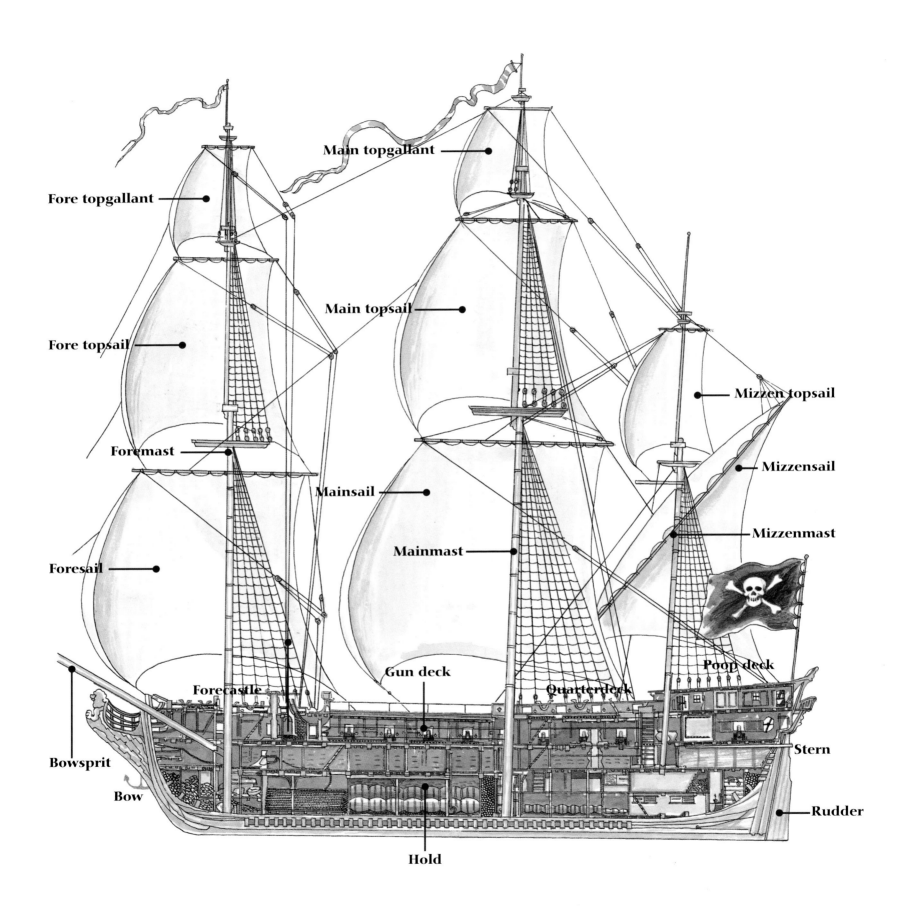

Fore topgallant

Main topgallant

Fore topsail

Main topsail

Mizzen topsail

Foremast

Mizzensail

Mainsail

Foresail

Mizzenmast

Mainmast

Gun deck

Poop deck

Forecastle

Quarterdeck

Bowsprit

Stern

Bow

Rudder

Hold

# PIRATE SHIPS

Pirate ships were certainly not all the same. Some were small oared galleys and others were larger three-masted ships that were more seaworthy on more open waters. Above all, pirate ships had to be fast, have plenty of firepower, and be loaded with bloodthirsty men willing to fight to the death. Pirates needed to attack their victims swiftly to take advantage of the element of surprise. They could not afford to spend days chasing their victims out on the open seas, so they hid in coves and other protected areas near common shipping lanes, harbors, and inshore waters, so they could attack the very instant a trade ship passed by.

Pirates could not build their own ships or order them from a shipbuilder because they were wanted criminals. Pirates were thieves, and most of their ships had been stolen from somebody else. However, pirates usually made similar modifications to their ships in order to make them better pirate ships. They strengthened the side decks to better withstand enemy fire and added large cannons and swivel guns for firepower. In the lower decks of their ships, they sometimes added barrels of rocks or sand for ballast. This put weight in the bottom of the ship to compensate for the weight of cannons and equipment above, so the ship didn't fall over.

Pirate captains and crews probably spent more time performing maintenance and making modifications to their vessels than they did committing acts of piracy. When they were not out attacking on the seas, they spent days and sometimes weeks repairing sails, making ropes, and scraping barnacles off the hull (called careening). When performing these tasks, they hid in remote areas, as they feared being caught by the authorities on dry land.

## ✳ OARED GALLEYS ✳

The Barbary corsairs used light, oar-powered galleys to attack larger merchant ships. These galleys were powered by slaves captured by the corsairs of Barbary and Malta. They were shackled together and forced to pull the galley's long oars, each of which required five men or more to move. Most galleys had a single, large mast that was hoisted quickly in the event that wind power was used.

Firepower for the oared galleys typically came from a large cannon mounted at the bow of the boat and several smaller swivel guns mounted on the sides. In addition to its weaponry, galleys had the advantage of being able to carry more than one hundred fighting men, whose strategy was to board and attack their unsuspecting victims.

## ✳ SLOOPS ✳

The most commonly used pirate ship in the Golden Age of piracy was the sloop. Although the word *sloop* can be used to describe many different vessels, a common sloop was much smaller than a schooner or merchant ship (called a galleon in the Spanish Main). Not much is known about the sloops pirates used, because they didn't keep records or diagrams of their ships. However, most of them probably used stolen sloops that originally had been built by shipbuilders in Jamaica and Bermuda for merchants in the Caribbean who wanted to avoid attacks by the buccaneers.

The only sunken pirate ship that has been firmly identified is Sam Bellamy's WHYDAH, which was discovered off the coast of Cape Cod in 1984. This particular pirate ship weighed over 300 tons and had 28 guns.

The construction of these sloops would have varied greatly, but most of them likely had two masts: a main mast supporting a large, square-shaped main sail and a smaller sail, and a foremast with only one small foresail. Some held as few as four to six cannons with several swivel guns, while larger ones held up to twelve cannons. These sloops had to be seaworthy enough to sail in foul weather, yet sleek enough to quickly overcome enemy ships.

## ❈ SHIPS ❈

Pirates, especially those who traveled beyond the Spanish Main, also captured and used large, bulky ships, similar to the galleons used by merchants. In the later days of piracy, especially in the late 1600s and early 1700s, pirates such as Captain Kidd, Blackbeard, and Bartholomew Roberts used large ships to carry out their raids. Pirates required larger ships for two main reasons. First, they had to have vessels with adequate firepower and crew to compete with British naval ships. Second, they needed large ships that were seaworthy and were capable of crossing large distances over rough seas.

This larger class of vessel was typically more than one hundred feet long, had three masts, weighed in excess of 250 tons, and carried more than 150 crew members. Some of these large ships were equipped to allow crews to oar them when seas were calm, but most probably did not. Similar in size to galleons, many held more than 30 guns, ranging in size from small swivel guns to larger cannons. Although not swift like a sloop, these ships had the firepower needed to attack larger vessels. Sometimes, large ships traveled in convoys with sloops. In one of Blackbeard's raids on the Atlantic coast of North America, he was accompanied by three sloops as he blocked and attacked passing ships.

## ❈ SCHOONERS ❈

Schooners were used in the later days of piracy, in the 18th century. A schooner is commonly a two-masted ship with fore and aft sails. Interestingly, the schooner is the subject of many fiction books and is the most common type of sailing vessel today.

# LIFE AT SEA

Life at sea for the pirates was harsh. Much of a pirate's time was spent waiting for merchant vessels to pass by, sailing from one place to another, or making repairs to the ship. Despite this, the seafaring life attracted pirates because it offered a life of adventure and the possibility of great riches instead of the boredom or persecution they would have experienced on land.

## ❈ CODE OF CONDUCT ❈

Many pirates lived by strict rules, called a Code of Conduct. Pirate ships operated like a democracy where decisions such as where to attack or how to take care of the ship were brought to a vote. Below shows a sample of what a pirate crew's Code of Conduct may have been:

I. Every crew member on the ship has a vote in all matters and has equal share to provisions, such as food and liquors.

II. Every man shall obey the chain of command, and all issues that arise pertaining to the decisions on the ship are held to a vote. The captain shall receive one full share and a half of all booty taken, and the other officers one share and a quarter. All men receive an equal share of prizes.

III. No man is to gamble at cards or dice for money.

IV. All crew members will keep their musket, pistols, cutlasses, and other weapons clean and ready for battle.

V. If any man should plan to abandon ship or run away, he shall be marooned with one bottle of water, a musket, some shot, and powder, or be put to death.

## ❈ JOBS ❈

Although pirates scoffed at authority and did not like being told what to do, there was surprising order to most pirate ships. There were defined positions on ships, and each position was voted by the crew.

The captain of a pirate ship was usually elected by the crew, based on his skill and strong leadership. Although the captain was technically in charge of the pirate ship, the crew usually had a say in deciding where to sail and when to attack. A captain could also be voted out by the crew and marooned. The captain's right hand man was called the first mate. The first mate assisted the captain and took over if something bad happened.

Quartermasters were the backbone of pirate ships. The quartermaster oversaw the daily operations of the ship, including directing attacks, deciding how booty was divided up, managing supplies, and directing work crews.

Surgeons were valued by pirates because they sometimes had experience treating the sick and wounded, but most didn't have real medical training. When an experienced surgeon was not available, the crew might elect a surgeon who they felt could do the job. Carpenters were also highly skilled at fixing and making modifications to the ships.

Often the ship's carpenter was the surgeon because he had
the saws needed to amputate infected limbs!

Navigators and gunners were important jobs on every pirate ship. The navigators had training to use delicate instruments and navigate the seas. Gunners were arranged in crews and spent much time mastering the maintaining, loading, and firing of the big cannons.

Most pirate ships had a cook. If a crew member could whip up a batch of savory turtle soup, he was qualified for the job. Pirates who had been wounded in battle and could no longer fight often served as cooks.

## ❋ ROUTINES ❋

Contrary to what you may have imagined, pirates were not always attacking ships and taking booty. Life on a pirate ship was often boring, with pirates occasionally waiting weeks for merchant ships to pass by.

A pirate ship required constant maintenance. Sails

ship, the crew would sail to a remote place, and run the ship aground on a sandy beach. Here, pirate crews would work fast and furiously, scraping and stripping the hull, and sealing the seams between the wooden planks with hot pitch before anyone could find the pirates and capture them.

## ❋ FOOD AND DRINK ❋

Pirate ships had no refrigerators or freezers to store food. One of the biggest problems pirates had with food was consuming it before it spoiled. For this reason, they did not have the luxury of regular fresh meat and produce on their ships, unless they caught some turtles, which were abundant in the Caribbean. When turtles were not available, pirates sometimes fished from their vessels. Pirates also collected wild animals like goats and birds

On long voyages, pirates ate hardtack even when it had weevils in it,
because it was often all the food they had!

needed mending after weathering a bad storm or from simply slapping against the masts. Ropes would rot due to exposure to sun and salt—or worse, rats chewing through them. One of the most demanding tasks that pirates faced was careening their ships. After spending weeks or months at sea, ships grew barnacles and seaweed on the hulls, which made them sail much more slowly. Also, little worms ate away at the wood, putting the ship in danger of sinking. To careen a pirate

to take on board while they were hidden near islands.

One famous food of pirates was hard baked biscuits called hardtack. These biscuits were made only of flour and water and lasted for a long time. But they didn't last forever! Sooner or later they would become infested with weevils, which are small beetles hatched from maggots.

Pirates also carried barrels of water on their ships, but it was consumed or went bad quickly. For drink, pirates loaded their ships with barrels of wine and bottles of beer, in part because the alcohol in the beverages helped to preserve it.

The pirates of the Indian Ocean captured luxury cargoes of spices, such as ginger, cloves, nutmeg, and cinnamon. These spices were valuable because they flavored food and also preserved it.

## ❈ MEDICINE AND DISEASE ❈

Pirates rarely had the chance to eat fruits and vegetables that contain vitamin C during long sea journeys. Because of this, many sailors developed scurvy, which is caused by eating too little vitamin C. When a pirate got scurvy, it was bad news. The disease caused the limbs to weaken and teeth to loosen because of swollen gums. It also affected connective tissues that hold the body together, like ligaments and tendons.

Pirate ships probably carried a very basic surgeon's kit that contained sharp knives, needles for stitching wounds together, and instruments to remove shot from flesh wounds caused by enemy guns. Even a small cut could become infected, and sometimes whole legs or arms had to be sawn off. Medicines were usually a combination of ointments made of spices and herbs. Because of the close quarters, disease was easily spread on a pirate ship.

## ❈ PETS ❈

Pirates may have had pets on their ships for companionship. Dogs and cats were occasionally kept on ship. Parrots didn't need to eat much and could be trained to talk, providing entertainment for the crew. The idea of every pirate having a parrot, however, is largely a myth.

# NAVIGATING THE SEAS

Modern cargo ships contain radar, communication tools, global positioning systems, and accurate maps, called charts, that allow them to navigate the seas easily. Ship navigators can even use some of these tools to study weather patterns and avoid dangerous storms that may be looming ahead. Pirates, unfortunately, had none of these high-tech gadgets to assist them in sailing the seas.

## ❋ MAPS AND PASSAGES ❋

Pirates usually attacked merchant ships that were sailing through commonly-used shipping lanes. The routes were well known, and the pirates would just lie in wait until a trade ship sailed by. Many pirates moved from place to place, so they had to have some knowledge of navigation and make sound decisions, or they would end up lost at sea.

The conquistadors of Spain sailed and charted most of the lands in the New World during the 16th century. Mapmakers, called cartographers, constructed detailed maps of land masses and seas that their ships explored. The captains of the Spanish galleons and other merchant ships used these maps to assist them in sailing from one port to another. The pirates were not as organized as the Spanish government, so they didn't have an organized system for making and sharing maps.

Pirates were, however, very good at stealing what they needed. Detailed charts stolen from captured ships enabled pirates to explore unknown waters and coastlines. These maps also provided pirates with information about the routes that merchant ships traveled, enabling them to plan future attacks.

## ❋ NAVIGATIONAL AIDS ❋

Although maps were difficult to come by, pirates did have access to common navigational instruments that were used to find the right direction when sailing the seas without land as a guide. Detailed charts were extremely important to pirates, as they helped determine an approximate fixed position in the sea. Navigational instruments were used to help pirates locate their position on a map. Many maps and charts had lines of latitude and longitude. Knowing the latitude helped pirates calculate their north/south position and the longitude signaled their east/west position. Using some of the navigational instruments on these pages, pirate navigators would take regular readings and plot the position of the ship on a map, enabling them to determine their location and distance traveled. These instruments weren't totally accurate and reliable, but they did give the ship's captain a good idea of where the ship was going. Pirates may have also used telescopes to sight land and wind vanes to determine wind direction.

The compass was probably the most important navigational instrument on the ship. It was used to determine the basic cardinal directions of north, south, east, and west. A compass has a small, floating needle that is magnetized on one side, indicated by an arrow. This magnetized arrow is drawn to a magnetic field near the North Pole, so it always points north.

Determining east/west position was most problematic for the pirates. They used an astrolabe to determine the ship's latitude. A pirate navigator would take two readings while looking through two small holes in the moving pointer of the astrolabe. First, the navigator calculated the height of the sun at noon. Second, he calculated the height of the North Star at night. The sun and the North Star (called Polaris) were fixed positions. Navigators knew that the further north they sailed, the higher the North Star would appear in the sky. It would appear lower on the horizon the further south they sailed. By taking these read-

ings and calculating the angle between their ship and the sun or North Star, pirates could determine their approximate north/south position. The main problem with the astrolabe was that it could only be used when the skies were clear, so the navigator could see the sun or North Star. Also, if the pirate ship was sailing in the southern hemisphere, the navigator would have to rely on the sun, because the North Star could not be seen at night.

The cross-staff was one of the earliest navigational instruments used to determine latitude. Like the astrolabe and the compass, this tool was difficult to use on

rough seas, as it required a steady hand to produce an accurate reading. The cross-staff was a
long staff, longer than a yard stick, which was
held on the shoulder and pointed at the
sun. On the staff were several cross-bars of
different sizes, which pointed up and
down when held to the sky. The navigator would choose the cross-bar that
closely matched the distance between
the fixed position, like the sun, and
the ocean. By sliding the selected
cross-bar back and forth until it
touched both the fixed body
and the horizon, the navigator

could convert the reading on the cross-staff to the approximate latitude.

Dead reckoning was a complicated process of determining how far a ship had traveled based on its speed. First,
navigators would determine their north/south direction.
The winds did not always move in the same direction as the
ship, so the ship had to turn back and forth to use the wind
to its advantage, allowing it to sail back and forth to
achieve the desired direction. This was called tacking.
Second, to calculate the speed of the ship, pirates may have
tied a small log to a rope with a series of knots in it. When
tossed overboard, the navigator would count how many
knots passed the hand against a minute hourglass to calculate the approximate speed of the ship.

# PIRATES
# ON THE ATTACK

When a merchant ship spotted the skull and crossbones and heard the boom of a cannon, they knew they were in trouble. Most pirate ships were fortified with extra cannons and often fired them when attacking another ship. The weaponry of pirates far surpassed that of their victims and they had more sailors to use the weapons. However, pirates had to be careful when they attacked, because they did not want to damage the other ship too badly. If the ship they attacked burned—or worse, sank—they would lose the booty they were trying to steal. And, if a captain thought the victim ship was sleek and seaworthy, he might want to keep it for himself.

Pirates had different methods of attacking ships. Sometimes pirates were sneaky and flew the flag of a friendly country to trick their unsuspecting prey. When the pirate ships were close enough to fire their cannons, they would raise the Jolly Roger, giving them the element of surprise. Other times, pirate crews made a lot of noise and looked mean and intimidating, waving shiny cutlasses and smoking guns. This "fear factor" scared the crews of merchant ships, and most of the time they surrendered without a fight.

## ❋ PIRATE FLAGS ❋

The Jolly Roger, known by many as the "skull and cross-bones," was the flag flown by many of the pirates. A hoisted Jolly Roger, with its intimidating image of death, instilled great fear upon the enemy crew that saw it. The origin of the Jolly Roger name is unclear, but many believe it comes from a French term for a red flag, called jolie rouge. Others speculate that it comes from a term used to describe the devil: Old Roger. Whatever the origin, pirates used these scary-looking flags to strike fear in their victims! Although the most common images of pirate flags contain a skull and crossbones (an image of death perhaps taken from grave-stones in cemeteries), Jolly Rogers also depicted swords, hourglasses, and skeletons.

Pirates were clever and deceptive, and probably carried an assortment of non-pirate flags on board, in addition to their Jolly Roger. To get close to the ships they wanted to attack, pirates would often fly the flag of their own country or the country of the ship they were approaching. When the pirates were near enough to attack, the command would be given to hoist the Jolly Roger. The sight of the Jolly Roger—and its terrifying message—was usually enough to make a crew surrender without a fight. Some pirates probably flew plain black and plain red flags: the red flag meaning battle, and the black flag meaning death to those who chose not to surrender!

## ✵ WEAPONS OF THE SHIP ✵

All pirate ships had cannons, but the number and variety depended on the size and type of pirate ship. Oared galleys used in the early days of piracy typically had one large cannon in the bow of the ship. Large, three-masted ships sometimes had more than 30 cannons. Cannons were of different sizes and shot balls of varying sizes. Typical cannons were built of thick steel and had fairly short barrels that enabled the crew to maneuver and easily conceal them. They were sometimes mounted on a wooden frame with a swivel in the center that allowed the gun crew to adjust the pitch, or how far the barrel pointed up and down. A tiered wooden wedge at the back of the cannon could be pushed in and out, and was used to brace the cannon once the proper pitch was set. Cannons shot large metal balls, which effectively busted down sails and broke up the timber of the victims' ships. Cannons were usually only used until pirates got close enough to board the enemy ship. Sometimes pirates fired a broadside shot, where all cannons on one side of the ship fired at once. The danger of a broadside was damaging or sinking the enemy's vessel, rendering it unusable.

Swivel guns were mounted on the ship and had short barrels. They were easy to maneuver and aim, but their range was shorter than the cannons.

Firepots were exactly what the name suggests: "pots of fire." Pirates filled clay pots with tar and cloth. These were set on fire and thrown upon an enemy ship, sometimes causing it to catch on fire. It also provided a smoke cover for pirates when they boarded other vessels.

A grappling hook looks like a huge iron fishing hook with three points, but they weren't used for catching big fish. These weapons had long, curved, barbed hooks and were tied to a rope. When a pirate ship sailed close enough to an enemy vessel, these hooks were thrown across to catch the rigging or other part of the ship. Using raw manpower, pirates could pull their enemies' ship closer to them, enabling them to board it and fight.

## ✵ WEAPONS OF THE PIRATE ✵

Weapons used by pirates were similar to those used today, but they were not as dependable. Muskets and pistols had to be re-loaded after each shot, were not extremely accurate, and often rusted because of the salty seas. Pirates usually carried many different personal weapons for each attack, just in case something failed or they needed different weapons for different situations.

The musket was a long rifle that was used to shoot the crew of an enemy vessel from a distance. In between shots, a pirate would have to manually load the musket with ball and powder. Its long barrel provided a fairly straight and accurate shot. Pirates didn't use muskets when boarding their victims' vessels since they were too long, clumsy, and took too much time to reload. They were impractical for the close combat pirates often encountered.

The flintlock pistol was the weapon of choice for many pirates. It worked much the same way as the musket, except it was light and short barreled, making it ideal for using when boarding a victim's vessel. Sometimes pirates carried more than one because reloading took time. When all else failed, pirates used the pistols effectively as clubs.

The cutlass was the favored weapon of the pirates. It was a sword that had a short, razor sharp, double-edged wide blade and a handle with a guard. Its short length was ideal for close combat on a ship.

Daggers were small, usually four-sided blades that ended in a sharp point. They were used for close combat where a cutlass was too long to swing.

The ax was a very versatile tool for pirates. Many axes had two steel sides, one a traditional ax shape with sharp edge and the other that looked more like a pick.

Axes were used for ship maintenance and splitting wood, but they were also used as a weapon to climb the sides of ships (similar to how climbers use ice axes), cut through ropes, or to attack the enemy.

CANNON

SWIVEL GUN

FIRE POT

MUSKET

FLINTLOCK PISTOL

CUTLESS

DAGGER

GRAPPLING HOOK

# TREASURE

Many people think pirates only attacked Spanish galleons loaded with chests full of gold and silver, making them rich beyond their wildest dreams. It is true that the large treasure ships sailed by the Spanish often carried gold and silver that was mined or plundered in Central America and taken back to Spain to be minted into doubloons or pieces of eight. But when pirates attacked their prey, they typically had no idea what goodies were in store. More often than not, pirates plundered cargoes that didn't hold luxurious riches. Though not as exciting as gold, these were also considered treasures for the pirates.

Gold and silver were plundered in their pure form or taken as doubloons or pieces of eight that had been minted in Spain. Silver pieces of eight were sometimes cut into smaller pieces. Precious gems and jewelry, like gold and silver, were great prizes for pirates.

Some ships kept their valuables in treasure chests that

pirates, and many of them contracted tropical diseases like yellow fever. Others suffered from serious infections as a result of simple cuts, which would have been easy to heal with modern medicines.

Weapons were crucial to a pirate's success. Pirates needed large cannons to add to their vessels and personal

Some pirates, such as Captain William Kidd, were rumored to have buried their treasures. Though this is possible, pirates most likely bartered or sold their prizes or stored them temporarily until they could return for them later.

were like modern safes. They were usually secured by a padlock or other device, which only temporarily slowed down the pirates from taking the riches inside.

Many other items, such as tobacco, ivory from Africa, olive oil, spices, and pottery, were prized by pirates around the world for their value. They could be sold or traded at a port eventually. Food and drink were some of the most basic essentials that pirates plundered from other vessels. When they found drink like wine or rum, they were especially pleased.

Medicine kits were of little monetary value to pirates, but they were an important prize that helped keep the crew healthy. Life on the high seas was rough on the

weapons like pistols, gunpowder, and ammunition. The salty ocean air caused pistols to rust out and malfunction, requiring frequent replacement. Ropes and sails were also targets of pirates, to help keep their ships seaworthy. Everyday maintenance to ropes and sails was crucial, and capturing these items enabled pirates to keep plundering with minimal delays.

Even the captured merchant vessel could be a treasure, if a pirate captain liked the looks of it. If the ship seemed like it would make a good pirate ship, the captain might keep it for himself, outfitting it with a crew and adding it to his fleet. Some pirates abandoned their current ship for a captured one, finding it more suitable for their needs.

# FAMOUS PIRATES

### ❋ HENRY MORGAN ❋

Sir Henry Morgan was likely the most famous of the buccaneers. He was born around the year 1635 in England and left at a early age for a life at sea. Eventually Morgan was granted a license as a privateer and sailed to the coast of Central America, where he successfully raided several Spanish colonies. In 1665, he returned to Jamaica.

In 1668, Morgan and his men raided Portobello, on the coast of Panama, capturing the Spanish forts and castles. Morgan and his men captured the town and threatened to burn it to the ground if the President of Panama did

any enemy vessel. Joined by French buccaneers in 1671, Morgan assembled several ships and over 2,000 fighting men and decided to attack Panama, an important treasure port for the Spanish. The defenders of Panama, who outnumbered Morgan's company, were no match for the battle-hardened buccaneers. The pirates stole whatever valuables they could from citizens, and tortured others to reveal where any other treasure might be hidden.

Although Jamaica celebrated Morgan's raid of Panama, England was upset because they were officially at peace

A lot of what we know about Henry Morgan (1635–1688), comes from the book THE BUCCANEERS OF AMERICA, written by A.O. Exquemelin, a buccaneer who traveled with him. Morgan sued the publisher of the book for libel, claiming some of the references to his ruthless brutality were untrue.

not pay a high ransom. Word from England came that raids on the Spanish had to stop, so Morgan took the opportunity to purchase some property and settle down. However, when the Spanish declared war on Jamaica, Morgan was put in command of seeking and destroying

with Spain. Spain wanted Morgan to be punished for his attack and destruction of Panama. He was brought to England, but he was never put on trial. Subsequently, Morgan was named Lieutenant Governor of Jamaica and returned there in 1674. He became ill and died in 1688.

## ❈ CAPTAIN KIDD ❈

Captain Kidd's legend survives today as a result of the publicity surrounding his trial and public execution, and his mythical buried treasure that has yet to be discovered. He was born around the year 1645. In about 1689, Kidd was outfitted as a privateer and he sailed to the West Indies to attack enemy ships in England's war with France. Afterward, he settled in New York as a businessman and politician, but in 1695 he sailed to England in search of another privateering commission. He was granted a Marque, backed by wealthy government officials who instructed him to sail to the Red Sea and attack and capture French ships that were disrupting trade.

finding enemy ships. Kidd ended up ignoring his Marque and attacking Indian ships, including several from the East India Company, a major trade partner with England.

By 1699, Captain Kidd was wanted by the government of England as a pirate for not following his orders. He sailed for the West Indies, were he sold most of his booty and purchased a sloop. With his remaining riches, Kidd returned to New York, and attempted to strike a deal with England for a pardon. Instead they had him arrested and brought back to England to face charges of piracy for attacking Indian trade ships. In 1701, Kidd was sentenced to death by hanging. His body was chained and hung at Tilbury Point

**Captain William Kidd was hanged on London's Execution Dock in 1701. On the first attempt to hang him, the rope snapped, and it took a second time to succeed.**

He was ordered to bring back any booty to the English government. Luck was not on his side, as many of his crew died from illnesses and they did not have much success

as a warning to would-be pirates. Some of Kidd's treasure remains unaccounted for, and many believe that he stashed it near Gardiner's Island. It has never been found.

## ❋ MARY READ ❋

Mary Read was one of a few known female pirates, and concealed her identity by dressing, acting, and fighting as brutally as any man aboard a pirate ship. Read's parents had a son, but her mother secretly became pregnant and gave birth to Read while Read's father, a sailor, was out at sea. When Read's brother became sick and died, Read's mother dressed Read in boy's clothes and disguised her as her brother.

After much family hardship, Read continued to pass herself off as a boy. She was sent to work as a foot-boy for a French lady, and then she enlisted on a man-o-war, a type of warship. Read ended up falling in love with a Flemish soldier who didn't know she was a woman, and eventually revealed her secret to him. They arranged a proper wedding and it was there that Read wore her first piece of women's

clothing, a wedding dress. Read and her husband were forced to leave the army, but their colleagues so admired them that they donated money to help them get started on their new life together.

Read and her husband went away to the Netherlands, where they opened a small inn. Business declined after the war, and Read's husband died unexpectedly, forcing her to flee. She again dressed in men's clothes and sought employment on a vessel heading for the West Indies. After returning home with her money running low, she took advantage of an opportunity to fight the Spaniards in the West Indies as a privateer. Like many other privateers, Read turned to a life of piracy. It was during this time that she raided and fought alongside another brave, disguised female pirate—Anne Bonny.

# ❋ ANNE BONNY ❋

Anne Bonny's childhood followed a very different path than Mary Read's, but fate remarkably brought these fearsome female pirates together. Bonny was born near Cork, Ireland. After a scandal that caused her family extreme public embarrassment, Anne's father took Bonny and her mother away to America to begin a new life. Once there, her mother died, and Bonny began looking after the household affairs. She married a soldier without her father's consent, and he disinherited her, refusing to give her any money. Anne and her husband then sailed for the island of Providence, a haven for pirates, to find employment. It was at Providence that Bonny met the famous pirate "Calico Jack" Rackam. Looking for a life of excitement, Bonny dressed herself in men's clothes and eloped with Calico Jack for a life of pirating.

After some time at sea, Bonny became pregnant. Since the crew did not know that Bonny was a woman, Bonny and Calico Jack knew that her secret would soon be revealed if she stayed on board. They decided that Bonny would live in Cuba until the child was born and Calico Jack would come back for her.

Later, Bonny returned to the pirating life and sailed with Mary Read at some point. Legend says that the two women were the most courageous members of the crew, and led the boarding of the enemy ships' decks to fight. Eventually, Anne Bonny, Mary Read, and Calico Jack were captured and put on trial. Bonny was disappointed with Calico Jack's lack of leadership and willingness to fight. She was said to have told him before his execution, "If you would have fought like a man, they wouldn't have to hang you like a dog." Calico Jack Rackam was executed and Mary Read died of fever in prison. No one knows for sure what happened to Anne Bonny.

## ❧ EDWARD TEACH, ALIAS BLACKBEARD ❧

Not much is known about Edward Teach, the famed "Blackbeard," but he was probably born sometime in the late 17th century in England. Around 1716, while privateering for England, he captured a French ship that he would make famous as his flagship, fitting it with more cannons and renaming it *Queen Anne's Revenge*. Blackbeard is best known for his daunting and fearsome disposition. He was said to be a large and menacing figure, and received his nickname from his long scraggly

more of the collected booty for himself, or to careen his ship and recover from a whirlwind year of plundering. Taking only the best of his crew and the majority of the loot on a small sloop, he marooned the rest of the crew on a small, uninhabited island. Then he sailed to Carolina and was granted a pardon.

However, Blackbeard was a pirate at heart and was soon back on the high seas. In 1718, the Governor of Virginia declared a proclamation to hunt down the pirate.

> During battles, Blackbeard carried several cutlasses and smoking
> pistols, and even lit matches under his hat to scare his victims!

beard, which was tied at the ends with ribbons.

Blackbeard was ruthless, plundering ships at will along the Atlantic coast of America. Once, he blockaded the harbor at Charleston, South Carolina to bargain for medical supplies for his men, also stealing gold and silver from the ships he took hostage. After that incident, Blackbeard sailed north along the coast, grounding his ship and one other. Some historians think he did this on purpose, either to keep

He sent two naval sloops to find him. One of the ships found Blackbeard near Orcacoke Inlet in November of that year, and a fearsome close-quarters battle ensued. The captain of the naval ship and Blackbeard faced each other in the fight. Blackbeard purportedly received 25 wounds before finally dying. The naval captain cut off Blackbeard's head and hung it on the bowsprit of his ship as he sailed back home.

## ❋ STEDE BONNETT ❋

Major Stede Bonnett retired from the King's guard to a life of good wealth and fortune on a large estate in Barbados during the late 17th century. Bonnett had plenty of money, was a snappy dresser, and was a well-educated and traveled man, unlike most of the pirates on the high seas. In 1717, he purchased the sloop *Revenge*, probably because he was bored with his retired life. Bonnett was known as the "gentleman's pirate" for his demeanor, the way he treated others, his educational background, and his fancy dress.

Bonnet and his crew sailed from Barbados to the coasts of North America. Here they plundered a few ships, but his crew quickly realized that he knew nothing about captaining a ship. During this time of restlessness they came in contact with one of Blackbeard's pirate ships off the coast of Carolina. Blackbeard convinced Bonnett to allow one of his crew members to take command of the *Revenge*. Blackbeard also suggested that Bonnett join him on his ship and that they share whatever booty they plundered.

Bonnett reluctantly agreed, leaving the *Revenge* to sail with Blackbeard.

While sailing with Blackbeard's company, they managed to attack and successfully plunder several ships. When Blackbeard learned of the opportunity for a pardon, he decided to take it and suggested that Bonnett do the same. Bonnett, with some of his crew, went to North Carolina to receive their pardons. Bonnett then received a Marque to fight in the war against Spain. When Bonnett returned to claim the *Revenge*, he found that Blackbeard had looted it. Bonnett returned to piracy and was able to plunder several ships, but was captured during a battle with privateer sloops in 1718. He surrendered after a lengthy fight, and was taken to Charleston, South Carolina, where he was found guilty of the siege of the harbor. In 1718, Stede Bonnett was put on trial and subsequently hanged for his crimes as a pirate. We'll never know why he gave up his cozy secure retirement for a life of piracy.

## ❦ SAM BELLAMY ❦

Captain "Black Sam" Bellamy was the captain of the only pirate ship that has been discovered and identified, the *Whydah*. During the Golden Age of piracy, many ships—including treasure-filled galleons—fell victim to unpredictable, severe storms because they didn't have modern—day radar and communication devices to warn them of foul weather. Historians believe Bellamy was a treasure hunter who searched for these lost ships, hoping to find valuables buried at sea. After a string of bad luck while searching for lost treasures, he and his partner turned to piracy instead.

Bellamy attacked and plundered many vessels, but his most remarkable capture was the galley *Whydah*, traveling from Jamaica to London. When Bellamy captured the ship, he was delighted to find it was full of money, gold, ivory, and other goods. In 1717, he outfitted the *Whydah* with more cannons and recruited a crew of about 150.

Bellamy eventually left the Caribbean for New England, capturing several ships and collecting booty. Most pirates treated their prisoners cruelly and often tortured or killed them, especially those who resisted or refused to cooperate, but Bellamy was different. He once captured a pirate ship and offered to return it to the captain. But Bellamy's crew was upset over this kind gesture, so he sank the ship, still offering to join forces with the defeated captain. When the captain refused, Bellamy left him alone on a deserted island.

Unfortunately for Bellamy, he encountered one French ship that he shouldn't have tried to attack. After thwarting a couple of deadly assaults, Bellamy managed to escape at night and headed toward Cape Cod to repair the *Whydah*. It was here that a fateful storm sank the *Whydah* along with its riches, ending Sam Bellamy's life.

# ✤ BARTHOLOMEW ROBERTS ✤

Bartholomew "Black Bart" Roberts plundered more than 400 ships during his lifetime, making him one of the most prolific and successful pirates in history. He started his life on the sea in 1719, working as part the African slave trade. Roberts went on to pillage ships in the West Indies and off the coast of Newfoundland, attacking and capturing several sloops and fishing boats. It is rumored that he didn't indulge in liquor like most pirates did, but his brutal antics made him a feared man. Roberts tortured prisoners horribly, instilling fear in his crew. After pillaging the ships he attacked, he often burned them.

Roberts managed to sail and plunder along the African coast, taking more and more ships as he went. Eventually, the British warship *Swallow* caught up with Roberts and his company of pirates. Roberts sensed the threat by the warship and sent one of his ships, the *Ranger*, to chase the *Swallow*. A battle ensued, and the *Ranger* was struck broadside, causing the pirates to surrender after losing many men. However, bad weather and rough seas prevented the *Swallow* from taking on Roberts directly. The stormy weather continued, but Captain Ogle was eager to attack. He tricked Roberts by raising a French flag, which caused great confusion. When the *Swallow* was close enough to fire the cannons, Ogle ordered that the British flag be raised, and the battle began. After an exchange of broadsides, Bartholomew Roberts was found drooped over a cannon, killed in the barrage. The rest of the pirates in Roberts' company surrendered, resulting in the hanging of 54 men.

# WHAT HAPPENED TO THE PIRATES?

During the early 1700s, organized governments had little control over piracy. Pirates in North America and the Caribbean had the advantage of being able to hide among the small islands, inlets, and rivers that these locations afforded. The Royal Navy of England had a great fleet of warships, but they were focused on fighting the French. Also, it was difficult for them to deal with pirates who were thousands of miles away from Britain. Colonial America had a few powerful warships that could easily defeat pirate ships, but there weren't enough to deal with the high number of pirate ships plundering its coast.

In most countries, there were no clear laws detailing punishments for captured pirates, other than laws in England that stated pirates had to be tried there, even though it was difficult to ship a pirate such a long distance.

The governments in Colonial America and England were aware of the pirate problem, and they took steps to deal with it. England, for example, decided to grant pardons to pirates who turned themselves in, meaning the pirate was forgiven by the government for breaking the law and wouldn't be punished. Some pirates took advantage of the pardons because they didn't want to face the terrible consequences of being caught and tried by the courts.

One of the most gruesome ways England and Colonial America dealt with captured pirates was to hang them in public. Pirates who were caught were imprisoned and quickly brought to trial. They were sentenced to death if found guilty. A special wooden f rame—called gallows—complete with a rope and noose was custom-built for each hanging. Hundreds of boats would fill the Thames River and spectators lined the banks and docks near London to witness pirates being hanged.

When pirates were caught and put on trial, they were usually convicted. Public outcry against piracy and the

> Some pirates' bodies—especially the famous ones like Captain Kidd—were placed in a full-body steel harness called gibbet chains after the hanging and hung along the shores for sailors to see as they passed by. This gruesome pubic display was a friendly reminder of what would happen to those who followed a life of piracy.

government's concerns that pirate attacks would cripple merchant trade caused many pirates to be hanged. However, though hundreds of pirates were brought to trial, scores more were never caught.

By the mid-1700s, there were fewer organized bands of pirates for many reasons. The advent of steam-powered ships enabled navies to "sail" against the wind and capture pirate ships that depended on sails for power. Also, navies like America's didn't require the use of privateers after the War of Independence and the War of 1812, so there were fewer "licensed" pirates. The large numbers of pirate executions during the early 1700s was another deterrent for anyone considering a career as a pirate.

# PIRATE MYTHS

Much of what people know about pirates is based on myths—unfounded beliefs about the life of pirates for which there is no direct historical evidence. Stories and films about pirates have contributed to most of our notions about pirates and how they lived their daring and adventurous lives.

One of the most common punishments we associate with pirates involves "walking the plank." Some believe that when a pirate broke a ship's Code of Conduct, he had to walk a long board from the stern of the ship into the menacing ocean below. We don't know if pirates were really

probably had animals like dogs as companions. They might have traveled with chickens, pigs, and other animals, but they didn't keep them as pets—they ate them.

Books and movies often show pirates burying their treasure chests and creating elaborate maps that hold the

> One pirate legend was probably true. Experts now think that pirates often pierced their ears and wore earrings because they believed it would improve their sight!

forced to walk the plank, but some books mention the possibility. The guilty pirate was more likely flogged with whips, thrown overboard, or marooned.

Writer Robert Louis Stevenson, who wrote *Treasure Island* in 1833, created the character Long John Silver, a fearsome pirate who had a pet parrot on his shoulder. The parrot would say, "Pieces of eight!" referring to the valuable coins sought by Silver. Stevenson's characterization of Silver and his parrot certainly added an interesting dimension to this pirate's life, but most real pirates probably didn't have talking parrots. Historians don't know for sure, but pirate ships

key to the valuable riches that will one day be found. Pirates probably didn't waste their time burying their treasure for a couple of reasons. First, treasure was usually divided equally among the crew, so each man got paid a share of the booty. Second, pirates liked to spend their loot when they went ashore. They probably didn't save much for the future. Today, treasures may exist in galleons or pirate ships that sank and have yet to be discovered. However, there is no real evidence that elusive treasures of gold and glittering jewels are buried underneath the white sands of remote islands.

# PIRATES IN FICTION

The mystery that surrounds the ruthless and daring life of the pirates makes them an intriguing subject of fiction. The Golden Age of piracy ended around 1725, but the life of pirates continues to intrigue writers and filmakers.

Probably the single-most documented resource on the history of the pirates is a book called *A General History of the Robberies and Murders of the Most Notorious Pyrates*, published in 1724 by Captain Charles Johnson. This book is supposedly a true account of the voyages and plunders of the most famous pirates, but no one is sure exactly who the author is! Many believe that he was a sea captain or pirate himself, based on his knowledge of the pirates and their language. Others think that he was a writer or journalist. One theory suggests that Captain Johnson was actually Daniel Defoe, a famous author who wrote the story *Robinson Crusoe*.

Written as a children's play by J.M. Barrie in 1904, *Peter Pan* is a magical story of a young boy who never wants to grow up. Wendy, who is entranced by Peter and his fairy friend, Tinker Bell, flies away with him to Neverland. A band of pirates, led by Captain Hook, also lives on the island, and they capture Wendy and other children. Captain Hook decides to make his captives walk the plank, but Peter Pan swoops in to push Hook off the edge of the ship and into the waiting jaws of a crocodile.

Many films have been made about pirates over the years, and many actors have jumped at the chance to play a

Steven Spielberg's 1991 film HOOK features an adult Peter Pan, played by Robin Williams. Captain Hook kidnaps Peter's children to Neverland, where Peter must relearn how to fly and save his kids!

One of the most well-known pirate tales is the book *Treasure Island*, written by Robert Louis Stevenson. In this story, the young Jim Hawkins gets his hands on a treasure map of the infamous pirate Captain Flint. Hawkins outfits a ship and sets sail with a pirate crew to recover the buried treasure. Some of the pirates, led by Long John Silver, turn on Hawkins in an attempted mutiny. Hawkins and Silver capture the treasure and head back to the ship, leaving the mutineers alone on the island. The story ends when Silver escapes one night from the ship with a portion of the treasure, never to be heard from again.

dashing, adventurous pirate or privateer. Some movies, including *Blackbeard the Pirate* and *Captain Kidd*, were inspired by real pirates. Others are fiction, but still feature real-life secondary characters, like Sir Henry Morgan in *The Black Pirate*. One actor who was well known for playing good-guy pirates in movies such as *Captain Blood* and *The Sea Hawk* was Errol Flynn. More recent pirate movies include *Treasure Planet*, an animated version of Treasure Island that takes place in space, and *Pirates of the Caribbean*, which was inspired by the famous amusement park ride at Disney World.

# PIRATE SHIPS DISCOVERED

**P**eople today think of pirates as romantic adventurers who led daring lives. Their true lives remain largely a mystery, and the facts we know about them come from limited actual accounts, legends, newspapers, and documents from pirates who were caught and put on trial. Treasure hunters—professionals who use documented accounts of pirate ships that sank—use modern equipment to search the ocean floors for the possible prize of lost treasures.

In 1984, history changed with the first documented discovery of a pirate ship, off the coast of Cape Cod, Massachusetts. Barry Clifford, a sea explorer, discovered pirate Sam Bellamy's ship *Whydah*. In 1717, Sam Bellamy and the *Whydah* met its fate and sank in a storm only a few hundred yards from the shore. All of the crew, except for two that managed to get to shore, perished in the storm.

Clifford began the search for the *Whydah* in 1983. He used a salvage boat and instruments to detect metal on the ocean floor in search for the ship's cannons. It was a year later, in 1984, that they lifted the first of the ship's cannons from the seabed, but at first they were not certain that it was from the *Whydah*, as many other ships have sunk off the shoals of Cape Cod. The most convincing discovery came in 1985 when the ship's bell, inscribed with the words "Whydah Gally," was brought to the surface.

Since the first discovery of the *Whydah*, many items have been recovered, including silver, gold, jewelry, and other wares. The expedition continues today to uncover artifacts of the lost ship.

Blackbeard's ship, *Queen Anne's Revenge*, may also have been discovered. The *Queen Anne's Revenge* was a ship captured for Blackbeard in the Caribbean in 1717. Blackbeard outfitted the sleek vessel to make it powerful and able to evade warships by adding a crew of nearly 300 men and increasing its guns from 26 to 40. After his famous blockade of Charleston Harbor in 1718, he ran aground on a shoal near Beaufort Inlet and sank. Many believe that Blackbeard ran the *Queen Anne's Revenge* aground on purpose so he could disband his crew, escape, and retire from piracy.

In 1986, the Florida-based ocean research company Intersal, Inc., in cooperation with the state of North Carolina, made the initial discovery of a large cannon from which many believe is the wreck of *Queen Anne's Revenge*. Circumstantial evidence, such as the recovery of other cannons, artifacts including navigational instruments and personal items, and a ship's bell dated 1709, place it in the time period when Blackbeard's ship sank. Although there were thousands of shipwrecks in this area up to the 20th century, scientists have been able look at things such as the time the wood was milled for the ship to determine that the discovery might be the *Queen Anne's Revenge*. The wreck remains today in only about 20 feet of water and efforts continue to find direct evidence that would identify it as Blackbeard's famous ship.

# ARE THERE PIRATES TODAY?

Piracy still exists today. Pirates attack several hundred ships world-wide each year. Piracy can also include the theft of intellectual property like computer software, or even skyjacking, which is a form of air piracy where a plane is hijacked.

Pirates today are similar to the pirates three hundred years ago because they want to steal loot from cargo ships or steal the ships themselves. Most modern day pirates are organized gangs that reside along the coastlines of areas where large cargo ships are known to travel, such as Southeast Asia. Most modern trade ships have small crews and do not carry large cannons and guns to defend themselves. These merchant ships typically travel on safe seas and have the advantage of radar and communications to help them if any trouble arises. However, the crews of these ships are small and are not in the business of defending their ships and fighting off pirates. Modern day pirates use

governments have taken steps to patrol the shipping lanes of some of the world's oceans.

Software piracy is another form of piracy that is a growing problem today. This form of piracy can include the illegal copying, distribution, and sale of computer programs. According to Microsoft's software piracy website, nearly $12 billion was lost in the year 2000 due to pirated software. People around the world take computer programs, copy them, and sell them to other people. The computer program may look like a normal one, but it is a counterfeit, which means it is not the original program produced and sold by the computer software company. The problem for software

Using high-speed powerboats, modern pirates quickly sneak up to large cargo ships, much as pirates did long ago with sleek sloops that sailed faster then slow-moving galleons.

the elements of speed and surprise. If they are spotted by the crews of cargo ships, a general alarm is usually sounded and the pirates quickly flee the scene, waiting for another opportunity to plunder.

In most cases, modern day pirates seek to loot a ship's crew of their money and possessions, forcing the officers of the ships they attack to open safes and hand over valuables from the ships' stores. Some modern pirates take the crew as hostages and demand ransom for their release. Pirates are able to attack quickly and get away, usually before help can arrive. Cargo ships are usually safest where

companies is they don't make any profit from counterfeit software. The problem for the consumer is that there is no guarantee the software will work properly, as there is no warranty for it. It is difficult to monitor people who copy software because it is a worldwide problem. The pirated software is sometimes sent to others over the Internet, making it hard to track down the people responsible for distributing the illegal software. A worldwide effort is underway to stop software piracy, but many countries have different copyright laws. In the United States, the penalties for copying and pirating software are stiff.

# GLOSSARY

**astrolabe**—A navigational instrument used to calculate the north/south position of a ship by using the location of stars and the sun.

**Barbary Coast**—The Mediterranean coast of North Africa. The Barbary corsairs operated from here.

**broadside**—When all cannons were fired on one side of a ship at the same time.

**bowsprit**—A large spar (point) sticking out from the bow of a vessel, which helps support the ship's rigging.

**buccaneer**—Originally from the island of Hispaniola and named after the boucan—a meat smoker—hese brutal pirates attacked Spanish ships in the Caribbean.

**careen**—The process pirates used to clean their ships. Careening was accomplished by grounding the ship in a remote location and cleaning its bottom by scraping off weeds and barnacles. Detritus on the hull of the ship created more drag, slowing the ship down in the water.

**cargo**—Goods carried by merchant ships.

**caulk**—As part of careening a ship, caulking involved waterproofing the hull by applying pitch to holes and seams.

**Code of Conduct**—These were laws that pirate ships adopted. Each crew member had a vote in all affairs, and the majority ruled. Some pirate ships operated much like a democracy.

**compass**—A navigational instrument which indicates direction by use of a magnetic needle that points to the north.

**conquistadors**—Spanish explorers (late 15th and early 16th centuries) who sailed and colonized the "New World," including the Americas, Mexico, and the West Indies.

**corsair**—Pirates of the Mediterranean. The most famous ones being based on the Barbary Coast of North Africa and on the island of Malta. Their governments authorized them to attack each other.

**cross-staff**—Another navigational tool that had a long bar with several cross bars. The navigator would choose the cross bar that best represented the distance between a fixed position, like the sun, and the ocean. By sliding the bar to make the two points touch, the navigator could calculate the angle and estimate the ship's latitude (north/south position).

**doubloon**—A gold coin minted by the Spanish, double the value of other coins. Doubloons were highly sought often by pirates for their high value.

**foremast**—The mast at the front of a ship.

**galleon**—A large Spanish sailing ship with three masts and large square sails, used to carry treasures from the Americas back to Europe.

**galley**—A small sleek vessel, sometimes with a single sail, that was powered by several pairs of oars.

**gallows**—A special wooden frame with support beams and a crossbar that held a rope and noose. It was used to hang convicted pirates.

**gibbet chains**—A steel frame with chains used to display notorious pirates on the shores as a warning to would-be pirates!

**hardtack**—A hard baked biscuit that was sent on ships and eaten by sailors. It lasted a long time because it was hard, like a cracker. Sometimes they got infested with weevils—small worms that rendered them inedible, but some sailors ate them anyway.

**Hispaniola**—The island that lies between Cuba and Puerto Rica in the Caribbean.

**Jolly Roger**—The name most commonly used to describe a pirate flag. Most of these flags had a black background with an image depicting skull and crossbones, or a variation thereof. Pirates had their own versions of Jolly Rogers.

**mainmast**—The mast at the center of a vessel

**marooned**—Pirates who broke the laws of the ship were sometimes marooned—left alone on a deserted island with few supplies as punishment.

**mizzenmast**—In a three-masted ship, the mizzenmast is the mast at the rear of the ship.

**navigate**—To calculate the direction a ship will travel, using instruments, maps, and common knowledge.

**pardon**—The granting of freedom or excusing of crimes without penalty or punishment.

**piracy**—Robbery on the high seas. Piracy today has taken on different forms, such as skyjacking and the piracy of intellectual property, like software.

**privateer**—Given a "Marque of Letters," or license from the government, these legal pirates were authorized to attack ships from enemy countries. Some privateers operated beyond the limitations of their contract and pirated anyway.

**rigging**—The series of ropes and pulleys that hold the sails to the mast of ship and help control them.

**schooner**—A popular vessel of pirates, they usually had two masts and were sleek, able to catch up to larger merchant ships. Schooners could hold plenty of cannons and go into shallow waters.

**scurvy**—A disease caused from lack of vitamin C. Scurvy affected the body's ability to hold limbs together and caused gums to become swollen.

**sloops**—Sleek sailing vessels that had two masts and a shallow draft, enabling them to sail in shallow waters.

**Spanish Main**—The hotbed for piracy during the Golden Age, where riches were plundered from the New World. This area included parts of Central and South America that were controlled by the Spanish, and later included the Caribbean Sea and surrounding islands.